Jo Jo Moreschi was a student at the City of Liverpool Community College, on the BTEC National Diploma in Photography programme, from 1996 to his graduation in 1998.

He won the prestigious Student National Fujifilm Award in Editorial Photography, for the college, in June 1998.

He now exhibits, and publishes work in London, and Plymouth.

'Plymouth Unveiled'
Nude Portraits Photographed by Jojo
Printed by Ümit Ülgen

DB PUBLISHING

The DB Publishing House
Unit One A, Birch House, Commercial Square, Leigh Street,
High Wycombe, Bucks. HP11 2QT
Tel: 01494 452627 Fax: 01494 526069

Reproduced by The D.B Publishing House
Printed by Seven Corners Press

This book is dedicated to: my mother and my brother, (the one for her love, the other for his money); my first photography teachers, David and Alan (for saying 'yes' when they could so often have said 'no'); all at the Plymouth Arts Centre and Spectrum Photographic Laboratories (for their sponsorship); John Pollex and the other friends and strangers who have shown me unasked-for acts of kindness, Robert Lenkiewicz (for being one of the greatest influences on my life); Trevor Grimsdale (for believing in the potential of this project); Anna Jones (for riding to the rescue on her White Charger) and to Mary (for choosing me).

cover 'm' on plymouth's mountbatten

Foreword:

Naked Plymouth - A City 'Unveiled'

The nude in art and the telling of a story are strong elements for any exhibition. The photographs by Jojo combine both in this striking body of work. Capturing the atmosphere of life in Plymouth, these images expose different scenes and emotions to the viewer, amongst them humour and tenderness, sensuality, solitude and community. Jojo is not only talented at unveiling the moods of his sitters, but also at revealing settings – whether interior or exterior – of great texture. The narrative that accompanies most of the images allows the personalities within the photographs to express what it is like to live in and around the city. Jojo's subjects tell their own story, offering views, which - like the photographs themselves - frequently vary in form and content. To borrow the city of Plymouth's own 'civic catch-phrase', Jojo's photographs offer the observer an entirely new 'spirit of discovery'.

Throughout the past century the power of photography - as well as the aesthetics - has been well documented. The photojournalism and socially significant images of Lewis W Hine, Dorothea Lange, Jacob Riis, Margaret Bourke-White and W Eugene Smith have chronicled our lives and landscapes. The great American cityscapes have been presented as misty monoliths by Steichen and steely urban sculptures by Stieglitz, whilst Dmitri Kessel and Ansel Adams have created art from the natural world by photographing monumental rural scenery. In portraiture Eve Arnold and Dorothy Wilding, McBean, Leibovitz and Snowdon have excelled. Life in action has been captured, perhaps most enduringly, by the great figures of the French 'narrative lens' Robert Doisneau and Cartier-Bresson. Some photographers have become celebrated for their nudes – Bruce Weber, Mapplethorpe, Duane Michals and Baly Hinter Wipflinger – and some for their allegories, from Rejlander in the 1850s, to the more contemporary figures of Maud Sulter and Calum Colvin. With this vast international heritage of photography behind him, Jojo has encapsulated several of these genres in 'Plymouth Unveiled' – portraiture and the nude, landscape and social-documentary, even allegory.

Although the largest city on the UK's southern coast, Plymouth has often been described as a big village. A strong community life and a high civic profile, combined with a long and famous history, give Plymouth a unique place in the nation's landscape. Jojo's project is also unusual in that a cross-section of 100 people in the city have been photographed naked for this visual essay on life. Other photographic social-documentary projects have been undertaken elsewhere, but never one quite like 'Plymouth Unveiled'. This publication and the exhibition in summer 2001 capture the essence of Plymouth lives.

Seeing Robert Doisneau (1912-94) at the opening of an exhibition of his work ignited my own interest in photography. At over 80 he was still working, capturing time on film. After a lifetime of observation, Doisneau said that you may spend a cumulative total of many years taking photographs and yet, when all the final frames are added together, they amount to perhaps only a few seconds in time. Jojo has committed many months to this project, recording people and places that reflect a moment in time. Technically superb and stylishly human his work is wonderfully showcased in this beautiful book.

Martin Thomas
Exhibitions Officer
City of Plymouth Museums & Art Gallery

CITY OF PLYMOUTH
MUSEUMS
& ART GALLERY
DRAKE CIRCUS PLYMOUTH PL4 8AJ
Tel (01752) 304774   Fax 304775

Introduction

I was born and raised in Plymouth, a city in the south west of England, which has a long and distinguished history that includes being the home of Sir Francis Drake and Sir Walter Raleigh; the port from which the Pilgrim Fathers set sail; the first region to elect a woman (Lady Astor) to the House of Commons; and one of the cities most devastated by the German Blitz in the Second World War.

However, to me it was just a grey place populated by grey people. I left as soon as I was able to, but returned after about 18 months. This has been the pattern of my relationship with Plymouth ever since (a few years here, several away, a few more here, again away). I don't know what it is about the place that makes me want to escape from it, nor can I understand what draws me back. I do know that it is an integral part of this project.

In October 2000 it will be twenty years since I left school. During my working life, I have had scores of jobs and two careers, but it was not until I was 32 that I found a vocation. In photography, I have a medium to express myself which feels absolutely right.

From the moment I picked up the camera, I have been able to explore my interest in things that are normally kept hidden and my fascination at documenting the extraordinary nature of the everyday.
The first self-initiated project that I undertook explored a community's relationship to a cemetery. For three months I photographed people that I found on Sunday mornings in Toxteth Cemetery in Liverpool. I made images which included families tending graves, individuals walking dogs and kids that had set up tents and camped overnight.

After this came "Strangers to the Spotlight", which was made up of portraits of all the staff who worked behind the scenes at the Liverpool Everyman Theatre, photographed in costumes or with props which hinted at their role within the organisation. It was exhibited in the foyer of the theatre, and subsequently purchased by it.

"Simon and St Brides" saw me documenting a month in the life of a large church with a congregation of ten and a vicar named Simon. I photographed a wedding, a funeral and lots of meetings and services. The photographs were exhibited in the church as part of a local festival before being purchased by it.
Finally, I moved back to Plymouth where I have exhibited, on two occasions, work made during the past three years. This work focused on traditional, figurative nude studies made in studios under the heading "Yesterday's Nudes".

Plymouth Unveiled is a collection of 100 men and women who live or work in the Plymouth area, photographed without their clothes either in their homes or in their favourite locations. Part social documentary, part formal portrait, part environmental nude, these pictures reveal more than just the bodies of the participants as well as providing an insight into their experience of the city that links them.

But how did it all come about?

In July 1999 I visited the city of San Francisco to attend a family wedding and promptly fell in love with the colour, energy and exuberance of the place.

Coming home was hard, and I spent a number of weeks mourning everything that Plymouth wasn't, before I determined to embark on a project which might help me find out a little of what it was. I decided that if I had been living in San Francisco I would want to combine my love of portraiture and nudes, and make a collection of naked portraits.

Though I considered Plymouth quite a conservative city, I decided to have a go and see if I could make it here instead. I plucked the figure of 100 out of the air as a nice round number and set about making notices that I put up around the town centre inviting people to "take their clothes off in the name of art". Not long after that I received a phone call from someone who had seen it and was happy to participate. We made an arrangement for me to photograph them and Plymouth Unveiled was born.

Although primarily interested in placing the subjects in their home environments, I saw that taking a number in their favourite outdoor locations might provide some variety and help show a little more of Plymouth. With these sessions I would establish why the person/s had chosen the particular setting and then we would try to find poses in which they somehow interacted with that environment. Once we had a pose that felt right to them and looked good to me, I would take the picture. I felt that the only information that I needed to accompany these images was the person's name and where, in relation to Plymouth, the photographs were taken. In addition to the viewer being able to gain an insight from the surroundings of the people photographed in their homes, it is important to realise that the poses in which they appear were created in collaboration.

After I had interviewed them, I would suggest ideas sparked by their answers to my questions, they would try out any they liked and then we would narrow it down to one or two in which they were photographed.

These were the questions I asked:

1   Why are you doing this?
2   Who are you?
3   What gives you pleasure?
4   What gives you pain?
5   Who do you admire?
6   What traits in others do you wish you could emulate?
7   What do you want to say about your body?
8   Who or what are the major influences in your life?
9   If there was a fire, what would you risk you life to save?
10   What would you like the image to communicate?

To accompany these pictures I decided to invite them to give their name, occupation and a statement about Plymouth.

My experience of Plymouth changed over the course of the nine months it took me to photograph the volunteers. As I travelled across the city and visited locations in its immediate vicinity, I discovered a lot of natural beauty and some fascinating architecture. I found 100 people willing to take their clothes off in front of a stranger and in doing so came to realise that under the conservative veneer there lurks some lovely liberalism.

Whilst you would have to stretch your imagination considerably to believe that Plymouth is in any way on a par with San Francisco, I now recognise that amongst all the grey here there are some very colourful characters, and for now at least I'm happy to say that it is my home.

Finally, I would like to thank all the people who agreed to be photographed. I made no selection, but happily worked with whoever presented themselves. In a world in which we are bombarded by images of what the fashion industry dictates we should look like, and where our culture is guilty of a high degree of body fascism, I celebrate the diversity of shapes that the individuals within these pages have and I hope that you can join me in finding something of beauty in all of them.

"The uncanny is not to be found in the exotic, but in the everyday"

(author unknown)

julia, dave and steve on the mount edgecumbe estate approx 1 mile west of plymouth

plymouth is a cultural desert.
rilito: student

there's not much you can say about plymouth. it's boring.
cileia: student

I came to plymouth against my will, but having been here for fourteen years it's
no longer the place I live, it's home.
lynda: optical dispenser

plymouth is great, I love it. I've lived here all my life.
andy: engineer

v and ruth in plymouth's central park

jacqueline and Ian in the fortesque pub on mutley plain where they had their first date

mike on plymouth hoe

plymouth is where I was born and I have a love hate relationship with the place.
I'm growing to like it more and more as I get older.
katherine: works in a perfumery department

plymouth..the most architecturally inept town I have ever been in.

tony: retired head teacher

I've lived here most of my life (from the age of
ten) if I didn't like it I wouldn't be here.
ray: caretaker

plymouth is a hole but its getting better.
naomi: busy person (with olive)

plymouth is very dirty but it's got a lot of good characters somewhere in amongst the crap.
julia: mother/arts and crafts person

I was born in plymouth, I've been away but I've always come back.
I don't really like it. I'd love to move but we can't afford it.
emmeline: mother
plymouth is nice in places but beautiful in most.
craig: forrestry worker
(with tirion)

stuart and russel on sheepstor approx 10 miles north of plymouth

plymouth is a city where the imaginations don't yet match the big skies.
martin: feature writer with evening herald

plymouth is a city growing up from being a garrison town.
stephen: gallery technician

plymouth is grey.
ed: graphic artist

plymouth is not boring, I think it's really good here, you've got the hoe and
new things being built up. there's lots for the kids to do.
mary: full time mum of 6 (with shanda)

lisa at shaugh prior approx 6 miles
north east of plymouth

plymouth is beautiful, there's no where else I want to go to live.
trudy: shop assistant

I love being by the sea and the barbican. it's my home and it's full of sailors!
bec: mortgage administrator

h

linda (with roffey and rusper) on slapton sands
approx. 20 miles south east of plymouth

plymouth is a good place to live, very much it's own sort of character and so much potential.
it's got a real sense of optimism.
pete: computer network engineer

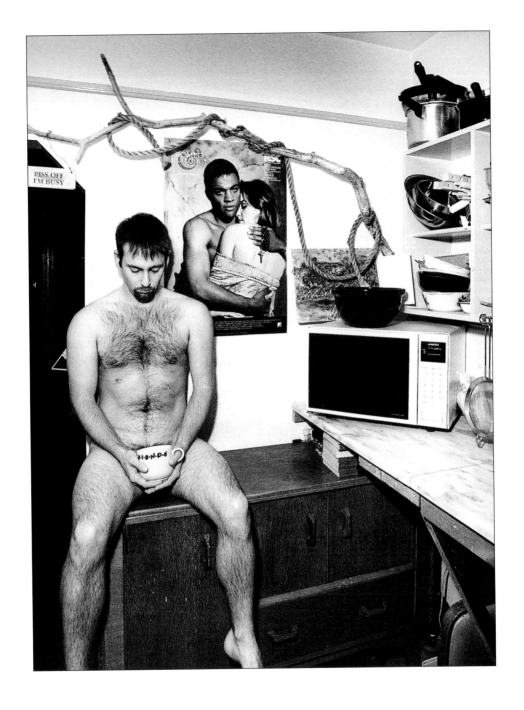

plymouth is my home and I love it, it's busy but not too busy, quiet but not too quiet.
rob: student

I adore plymouth. I've moved 29 times in my life and this is where I finally settled.
sandy: law student

I was born here so I find it hard to have an opinion about the place. I've lived away a lot but have always met interesting people in plymouth. a lot of people come back like homing pigeons without knowing why.

jim: *e.f.l.teacher*

I've lived here all my life, so I've got to appreciate it really, though it's going down hill rapidly.
mike: retired biomedical scientist

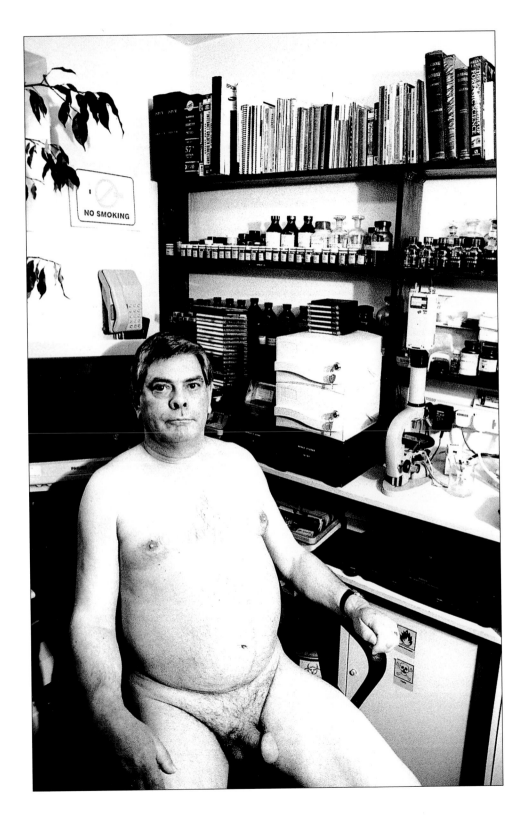

plymouth is a really nice place to live, you can have a modicom of cosmopolitan life and yet if you need to you can escape to the beach, the moors or cornwall there is a nice under current of alternative culture and creative people doing interesting things.
louise: midwife/singer/drummer

plymouth is very seasidey. especially my road. I enjoy the arts on the barbican and it's very oldy worldy as well.

sam: artist

It's a city of paradoxes: on the surface it's straight and rightwing but every aspect of life is here. there are all sorts of sub cultures hidden under the surface.

nik: pilgrim

whilst the pace of plymouth is like a town it has the opportunities of a city.
rachael: mother/potter (with daisy)

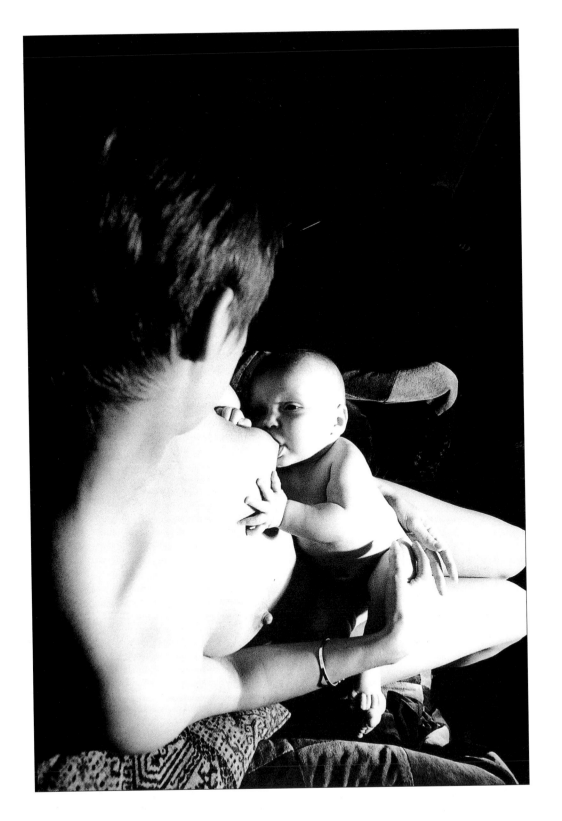

I was born and bred here with a mum and dad that were pillars of our community, (dad was one of the fishermen on the barbican) plymouth is a nice holiday centre for people to stop off in.

liz: dying

plymouth is slow and fresh and home.
danny: process operator

I like plymouth because it's close to the moors and close to the sea.
eddie: coach painter

I love plymouth, though it's fairly straight and conservative on the surface, underground there are great music, festival and party scenes alive and kicking. you can always find work here, it's a multi-cultural city with a really chilled vibe.

harry: analytical chemist/carpenter/minstrel

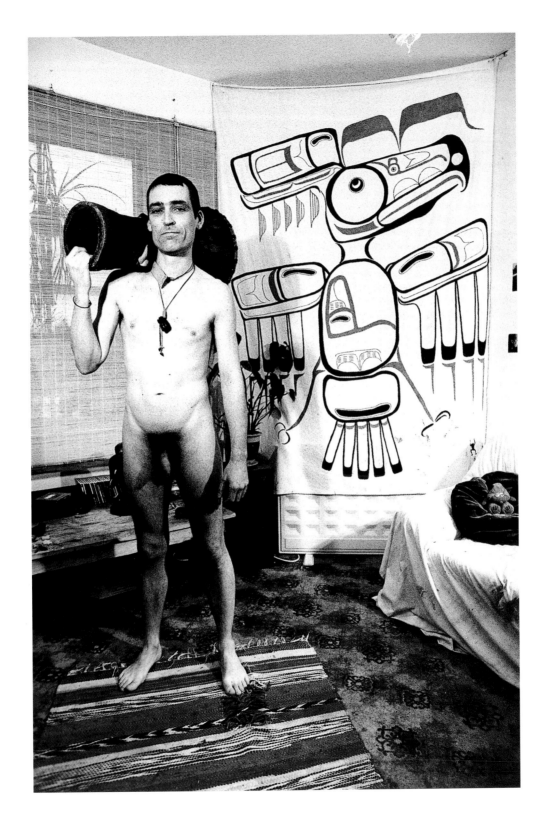

jane in a puddle next to burrator resevoir.
approx 10 miles north of plymouth

gareth on sheepstor approx 10 miles north of plymouth

plymouth is a good location to get to lots of beautiful countryside and coastline.

richard: landowner

I could say that it's better than any other city that I've been to recently. plymouth is a happening place.

dominic: art student

plymouth is my hometown. a home with one amazing garden around it and a home that has taught me how to learn.

maureen: retired primary school teacher and ocarina player

(with lucien)

plymouth is wet. when you're away you want to come here, when you're here you want to get away.
martin: quality inspector
plymouth is my sanctuary.
karen: acedmic administrator

life is a damn site better in the west country than it ever was in london.
katherine: part time student/volunteer

plymouth has got so much potential, why is it never used ?
nick: sports instructor

plymouth: it's like somebody without focus.
robin: unemployed

plymouth hasn't got brad pitt in it. It lacks confidence I think that everyone in plymouth should
take a leap of faith and get into the new century with a 'go get it' attitude.

heather: manager

I've been here for four years, it would be nice to go somewhere else, but if the job lands here I stay.
paul: cad technician

matt, andy, mandy, pat, marianne and steve
(members of the plymouth motorcycle club)
at the lee moor junction approx 10 miles
east of plymouth

I moved here over six months ago having lived in the south east for two decades. there's a better quality of life down here, people are much more friendly and out going and the bus drivers even say please and thank you. Its a genuine thing.

gazza: restorer

plymouth was where my soul was born. I'm a 'janner' and proud of it.

tanya jane: lifeguard/photography student

plymouth: rainy!
max: youth worker

plymouth is a really nice place.
maria: assistant manager in an indian restaurant

ray in his antiquarian bookshop on plymouth's barbican

mike, (in his city centre record shop) with andy

chris in a city centre car park

to live by the sea and not enjoy it is a crime.
keith: sailor

basically I have a love/hate relationship with the place, it's my home, I was born here. I'm a plymothian.
martin: freelance drama tutor

I don't really think that plymouth is a nice city but it's location is marvellous, nevertheless my home is where my heart is and mine is here. It's just not the most exciting city in the world.
ümit: photographer/chef

plymouth is an excitingly peaceful city.

colin: semi-retired

plymouth's got history, I really like it. I'm glad I came down here. I think it's a lovely place.

roz: housewife

plymouth holds a certain greyness locked in the stone and latterly the concrete sadly used to rebuild it. The hoe and the barbican hold the city's heart and hope which is huge.

mark: theatre artistic director

plymouth is a wonderful place which is slowly getting better, but where there could be so much more opportunity with vision from central county council.

jules: dance practitioner

plymouth is quiet, nice, bloody cold and wet.
beatriz: actress

plymouth is a wonderful place to live, there is so much potential. It is the heart of my world and everything else is a long way away. we are not along way from anywhere.

linda: unemployed

plymouth…'spirit of discovery'. it's a new beginning for me.
tracey: seamstress

simon at barn park road allotments in the city

plymouth has been the setting of many changes in my life, I will remember it because my personality varied a lot while I was here. but I won't stay here. I have other places to see.
william: photographer

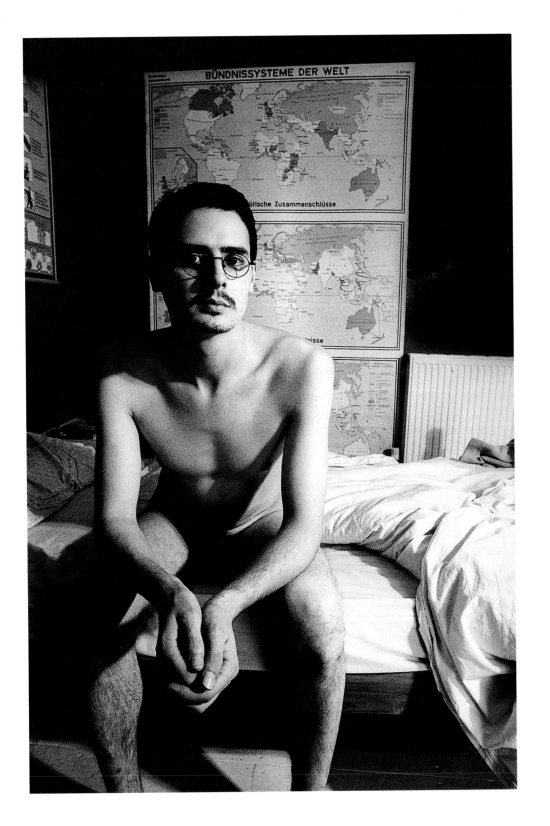

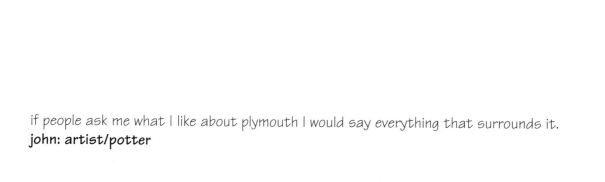

if people ask me what I like about plymouth I would say everything that surrounds it.
john: artist/potter

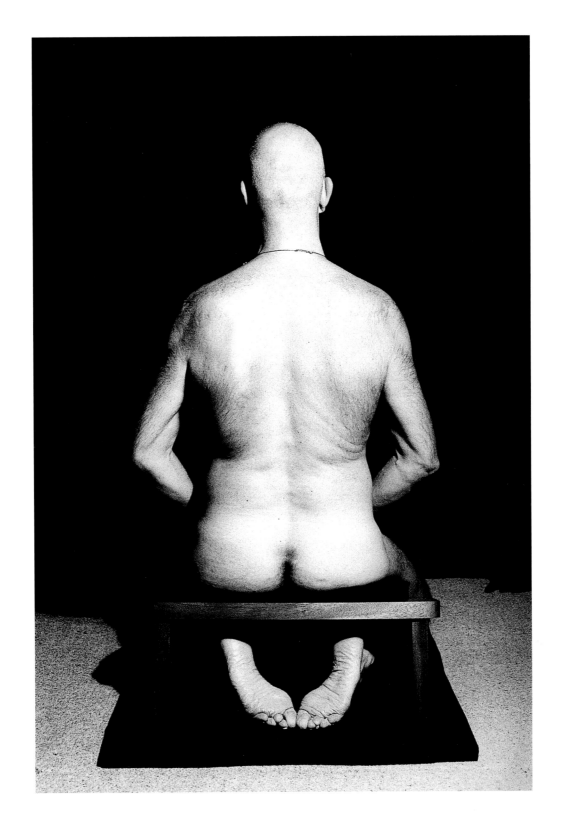

plymouth is the armpit of bristol.
jill: artist/mother/teacher

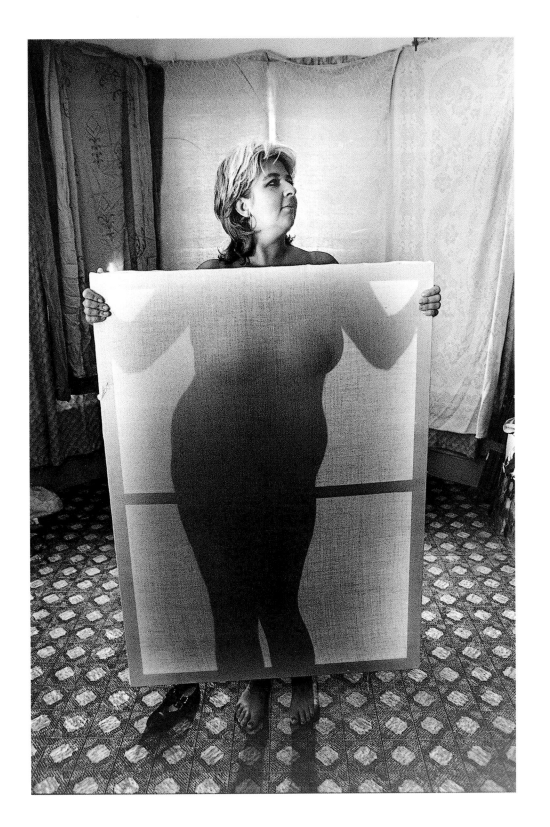

I think that people put plymouth down, I've moved back after living away for
12 years and being here makes me happy. It is my home.
mary: healer

plymouth is depressed but with hope.
jane: radiographer

plymouth is a city with a grey negative crust
that needs picking off, once you have there are
some very interesting people here.
juliet: radiographer/artist

It's a lovely place to live I have been down here 25 years and I love the area.

jack: In the navy

I've lived here all my life. I can't think of living anywhere else because I like living by the coast.

chris: housewife/mother

plymouth; it's home.
zoë: marine biologist
I came here for three years and got stuck.
rich: photographer

I love plymouth because there are a lot of good people here, but they're hard to find. there's a vibrant underground scene, but it's not very visible.

clare: massage therapist

I don't really like the military side of plymouth it's homophobic and racist. anybody different they don't like. but I love the countryside.

ursula: actress

I've travelled around europe and canada but I like it here. I've seen some good places and some bad places but I think plymouth is very beautiful.

bob: father of six

I don't like plymouth very much, it's going down the dumps. It's not like it used to be.

arthur: unemployed

(with ben, between his dad and grandad)

jane at black penny point approx 9 miles east of plymouth

what I like about plymouth is that it's safe compared to most cities,
and the west country is very beautiful to look at.
brenda: retired civil servant

john playing golf on a course in yelverton,
approx 6 miles south west of plymouth.

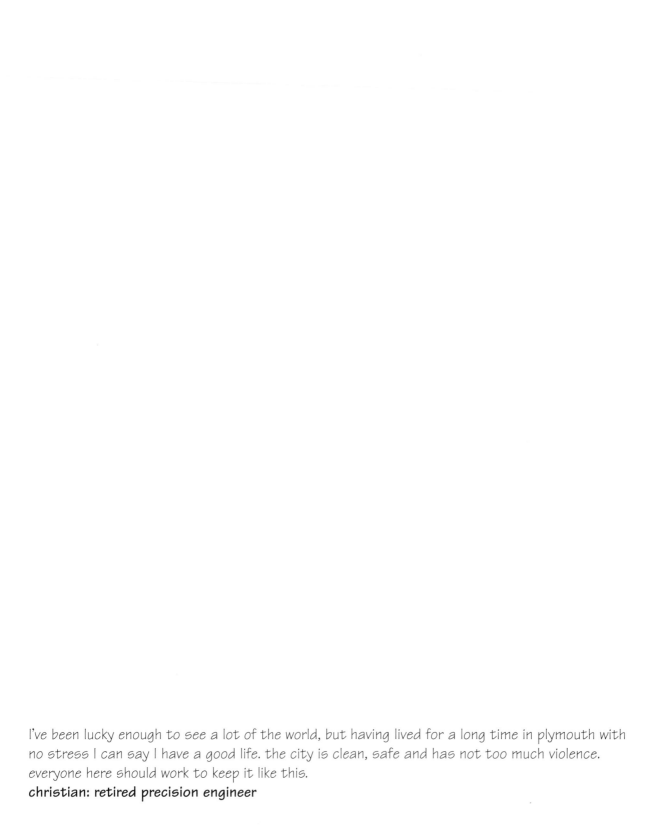

I've been lucky enough to see a lot of the world, but having lived for a long time in plymouth with no stress I can say I have a good life. the city is clean, safe and has not too much violence. everyone here should work to keep it like this.

christian: retired precision engineer

plymouth may be changing for the better at last.
mike: film editor

elaine in the grounds of saltram house in plymouth.

plymouth; it rains all the bloody time.
v: barmaid

the real plymouth is the barbican the city centre is a crib from scandinavian design. regardless of politics there seems to be a lack of awareness of the timelessness of the barbican.

jack: property developer

plymouth is like poland in the 1970's.

jules: reporter

plymouth is inward looking, not outward looking; from the water everything is grey.

andy: boat builder

plymouth is different to anywhere else that I've lived. I fell in love with it the minute I got here.
ruth: civil servant

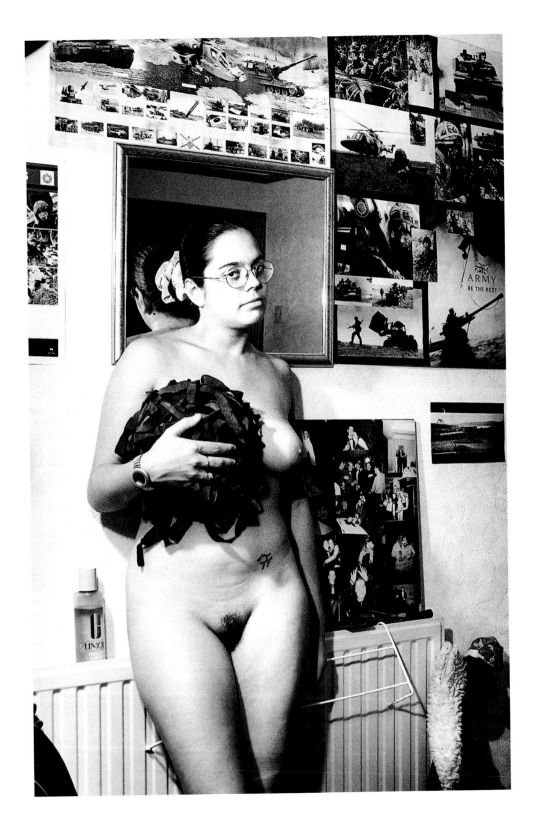

sam and nik on plymouth's barbican.